BREAST CANCEI

BEGINNERS

AN ONCOLOGIST RECIPES AND CANCER DIET RECOMMENDATION FOR BEGINNERS

Dr. Samuel Jackson

An instance of cancer that affects the breast flesh is breast cancer. A
tumor forms when cells in the breast begin to grow uncontrollably and
create a mass or lump...33

INTRODUCTION

Breast cancer is a difficult diagnosis that affects countless women around the world. It's a journey that can be filled with fear, uncertainty, and doubt. But it's also a journey of hope, resilience, and strength. The story of one woman's breast cancer recovery which was triggered by reading and following this diet cookbook illustrates just that.

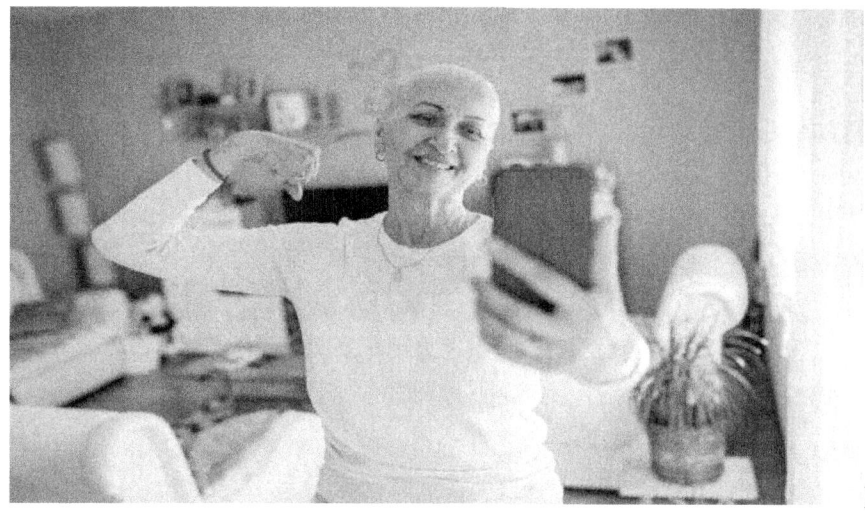 Maggie was an active and healthy woman who loved to hike and spend time outdoors. She had always taken care of her health and never expected to be diagnosed with breast cancer. But in 2018, Maggie was diagnosed with Stage II breast cancer.

She underwent surgery and several rounds of chemotherapy, which took a toll on her body and left her feeling weak and depleted. But Maggie refused to let cancer defeat her. She began to focus on her nutrition, researching the best foods to eat to support her body during cancer treatment.

Through her research, Maggie discovered this book you are currently reading and as aresult she began to understand the importance of a cancer-fighting diet that included plenty of fruits, vegetables, lean proteins, and healthy fats. Through this book, she found a new appreciation for cooking and began experimenting with the recipes mentioned in this cancer diet cookbook that were both nutritious and delicious.

Slowly but surely, Maggie's health began to improve. She regained her strength and energy and was able to return to hiking and enjoying the great outdoors. She knew that her cancer journey was far from over, but she felt empowered knowing that she was taking an active role in her own recovery.

Maggie's story is a powerful reminder of the importance of a healthy diet in cancer recovery. This cancer diet cookbook for beginners is a tool that has helped others like Maggie take control of their health and recovery. This cookbook provides you with valuable information on the best foods to eat during cancer treatment and includes easy and delicious recipes to help make healthy eating a breeze.

Whether you're a breast cancer patient, survivor, or caregiver, this cookbook is an essential resource for anyone looking to support their health through nutrition. Maggie's journey is proof that with the right mindset, support, and resources, anything is possible

Introducing the Cancer Diet Cookbook for Beginners - your ultimate guide to supporting your health and recovery through nutrition.

If you or someone you love has been diagnosed with cancer, you know how overwhelming the journey can be. But the right nutrition can make all the this particular cookbook provides you with the knowledge, tools, and recipes you need to fuel your body with the nutrients it needs to heal.

This cookbook is designed specifically for cancer patients and survivors. It includes easy-to-follow recipes that are delicious, nutritious, and tailored to support your body during cancer treatment. Whether you're dealing with nausea, fatigue, or taste changes, our recipes are designed to help you manage your symptoms and keep your body strong.

The Cancer Diet Cookbook for Beginners also provides you with valuable information on the best foods to eat during cancer treatment. I have done the research for you, so you can rest assured that the foods you're eating are supporting your body's healing process.

This cookbook is not just about what you eat, but also about how you eat. We provide you with tips and strategies for managing nutrition during cancer treatment, so you can feel confident and empowered on your journey to recovery.

Don't let cancer control your life. Take control of your health and recovery with the Cancer Diet Cookbook for Beginners. Get it now and start fueling your body with the nutrients it needs to heal.

CHAPTER 1

THE DYNAMICS OF BREAST CANCER

Breast cancer is a form of cancer that develops in the breast tissue. It is one of the most common malignancies diagnosed in women,. Breast cancer occurs when abnormal cells proliferate and multiply in the breast tissue, forming a tumor. If left untreated, these cancer cells can spread to other regions of the body, including the lymph nodes, lungs, liver, and bones.

There are several forms of breast cancer, including ductal carcinoma, lobular carcinoma, inflammatory breast cancer, and Paget's disease of the breast. Ductal carcinoma is the most prevalent type of breast cancer and develops in the cells that line the milk ducts. Lobular carcinoma develops in the cells that generate milk, while inflammatory breast cancer is a rare and aggressive form of breast cancer that can cause the breast to become red and swollen.

Breast cancer is usually diagnosed through a combination of imaging tests, such as mammograms, ultrasounds, and MRIs, and a biopsy, which involves removing a sample of breast tissue for examination under a microscope. Once diagnosed, the stage and grade of the malignancy are determined, which will help to guide treatment options.

Breast cancer is treated using a combination of surgery, radiation therapy, chemotherapy, hormone therapy, and targeted therapy. The form of treatment will depend on the stage and grade of the cancer, as well as other factors such as the age and overall health of the patient.

Surgery is often the first line of treatment for breast cancer and involves removing the tumor and any adjacent tissue that may contain cancer cells. This may be followed by radiation therapy, which employs high-energy radiation to kill cancer cells and shrink tumors.

Chemotherapy is another prevalent treatment for breast cancer and involves using drugs to kill cancer cells throughout the body. Hormone therapy is used to treat hormone receptor-positive breast cancer, which accounts for about two-thirds of all breast cancer cases. This form of therapy blocks the hormones that fuel the growth of cancer cells.

Targeted therapy is a newer form of treatment for breast cancer that specifically targets the cancer cells and is less likely to harm healthy cells. This form of therapy may be used in combination with other treatments, such as chemotherapy.

Breast cancer can have a significant impact on a person's physical, emotional, and mental well-being. It is crucial for patients to have a strong support system, including friends, family, and healthcare professionals, to help them navigate through the diagnosis and treatment process.

Lifestyle changes such as maintaining a healthy diet, exercising routinely, and reducing stress can also help to improve outcomes and reduce the risk of recurrence. Patients should also follow up with their healthcare team regularly to monitor their progress and resolve any concerns or side effects of treatment.

Breast cancer is a complex and potentially life-threatening disease that requires prompt and aggressive treatment. However, with early detection and appropriate treatment, many patients are able to attain successful outcomes and lead full and active lives. It is crucial for newly diagnosed patients to educate themselves about their options and to work closely with their healthcare team to develop a personalized treatment plan.

CAUSES OF BREAST CANCER

An instance of cancer that affects the breast flesh is breast cancer. A tumor forms when cells in the breast begin to grow uncontrollably and create a mass or lump.

The chance of developing breast cancer can be raised by a number of factors, such as:

Gender: Women are more likely than males to develop breast cancer.

Age: As people age, their chance of breast cancer rises.

Family history: Women who have a past of breast cancer in their family, especially in a mother, sister, or daughter, are more likely to contract the illness.

Genetics: Breast cancer risk can be raised by mutations in specific genes, such as BRCA1 and BRCA2.

Hormones: The hormones progesterone and estrogen, which are produced by the ovaries, can help some breast cancers develop.

Lifestyle factors: A number of lifestyle choices, including drinking alcohol, being overweight, not exercising regularly, and being exposed to certain chemicals, may increase the risk of getting breast cancer

Surgery, radiation treatment, chemotherapy, and hormone therapy are all options for treating breast cancer. The course of therapy is determined by a number of variables, including the cancer's stage, the patient's age, general health, and the presence of any genetic mutations. Working closely with your medical team will help you create a therapy strategy that is appropriate for your needs.

Breast Cancer Types And Stages

Breast cancer can come in a variety of forms and phases, which can impact both the prognosis and course of treatment.

Breast Cancer Types

A non-invasive form of breast cancer called ductal carcinoma in situ (DCIS) develops in the milk tubes of the breast.

Breast cancer that begins in the milk ducts and spreads to the nearby breast tissue is known as invasive ductal carcinoma (IDC).

A form of breast cancer called invasive lobular carcinoma (ILC) develops in the breast's milk-producing lobules.

A uncommon and aggressive form of breast cancer known as Inflammatory Breast Cancer (IBC) causes the breast to swell, turn red, and feel warm to the touch.

Breast cancer that screens negative for the ER, PR, and HER2/neu receptors is referred to as triple-negative breast cancer.

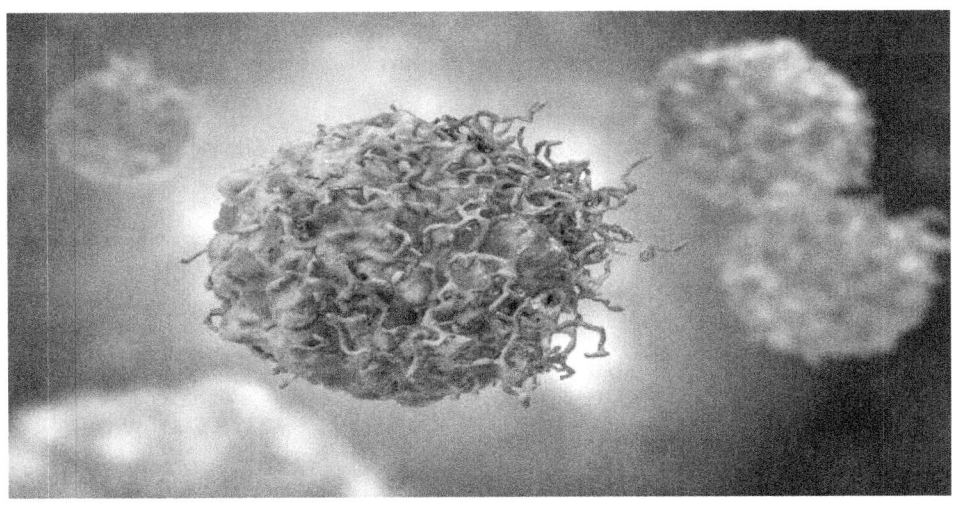

Breast Cancer Stages

The size of the tumor and whether it has spread to adjacent lymph nodes or other body parts determine the stage of breast cancer. These are the phases:

Stage 0: DCIS, wherein only the breast's milk ducts are discovered to contain cancer cells.

Stage 1: A minor breast tumor that has not yet spread to the lymph glands.

Tumor has grown and may have spread to adjacent lymph nodes in stage 2.

Stage 3: The tumor has expanded to the lymph nodes and has encroached on the skin or the chest wall.

Stage 4: The cancer has moved to the bones, liver, or lungs, among other organs.

It's crucial to keep in mind that every instance of breast cancer is different, and the prognosis and treatment will depend on the type and stage of the cancer. Having a close relationship with a medical team can help guarantee the best result.

EARLY CANCER DETECTION AND TREATMENT

For a person's prognosis and survival, early breast cancer detection and therapy are essential. The likelihood of successfully treating cancer increases with early detection of the disease.

The significance of early detection

Greater chances of long-term survival: When breast cancer is discovered early, these odds of successful treatment are significantly increased.

a less intrusive procedure: Instead of more extensive surgery or mastectomy, early detection of breast cancer provides for less invasive treatment choices, such as breast-conserving surgery.

Less aggressive treatment: If breast cancer is discovered early, less aggressive choices for treatment may be available, such as chemotherapy or radiation therapy with lower doses.

A person's quality of life can be enhanced by early diagnosis and treatment of breast cancer, which can lessen its physical and psychological toll.

The Value of Early Intervention

impedes the spread of malignancy Early intervention can help control the development and spread of cancer, which can enhance the effectiveness of treatment.

Additional treatment alternatives A wider variety of treatment options, such as surgery, radiation therapy, chemotherapy, and targeted therapy, are possible with early diagnosis.

Increased survival rates: Research has shown that early therapy of breast cancer increases survival rates when compared to delayed treatment.

Better odds of breast conservation: Choosing breast conservation surgery over mastectomy may be an option for early treatment, preserving the breast and enhancing body image.

The best outcomes, the preservation of quality of life, and the reduction of treatment costs all depend on the early diagnosis and treatment of breast cancer. You must take charge of your breast health as a woman by getting regular checkups and screenings to ensure early identification and, if required,treatment.

CHAPTER 2

NUTRIENTS FOR BREAST CANCER PATIENTS

Proper nutrition is crucial to the therapy and recovery of breast cancer patients. Eating a healthy, balanced diet that contains all the nutrients the body needs can strengthen the immune system, speed up recovery, and lower the risk of complications.

The following is a thorough list of the nutrients you should emphasize in your diet:

Protein: A necessary nutrient, protein aids in the development and repair of tissues, including those harmed by cancer therapy. The best sources of protein for breast cancer patients to eat are lean meats, poultry, seafood, beans, nuts, and seeds.

Carbohydrates: Because they give the body energy, complex carbohydrates like those found in whole grains, fruits, and vegetables are crucial for breast cancer patients to ingest. These foods contain a lot of fiber as well as vital vitamins and nutrients that promote general health.

Healthy lipids, like omega-3 fatty acids, are crucial for people with breast cancer. Omega-3s have been shown to enhance immune system performance and reduce inflammation. Healthy fats can be found in fatty seafood, nuts, seeds, and avocados.

Vitamins: The body requires a small amount of vitamins in order to operate properly. Patients with breast cancer should concentrate on eating foods high in vitamins, such as leafy greens, fruits, and veggies. Particularly essential for bone health and possibly contributing to breast cancer prevention is vitamin D.

Minerals: Minerals are necessary for a variety of bodily processes, such as the generation of energy, the immune system, and healthy bones. Patients with breast cancer should concentrate on eating foods high in minerals, such as whole cereals, lean meats, dairy, nuts, and seeds. For healthy bones, calcium, magnesium, and zinc are especially crucial.

Water: It's important for breast cancer patients to stay hydrated, particularly while receiving treatment. Dehydration, which can result in tiredness and other negative effects, can be prevented by drinking plenty of water and other fluids.

It's crucial that you collaborate with a registered dietitian or nutritionist to create a custom nutrition plan that caters to their unique requirements. Patients with breast cancer may benefit from nutritional supplements like vitamin D, calcium, and omega-3 fatty acids in addition to consuming a balanced diet.

Make eating a nutritious, well-balanced diet a top priority to strengthen your immune system, speed up recovery, and lower your risk of problems. A dietitian or nutritionist can assist in creating a personalized dietary plan that caters to their particular requirements.

ESSENTIAL NUTRIENTS AND THEIR IMPLICATIONS IN THE PREVENTION AND TREATMENT OF BREAST CANCER

A complex illness that affects a lot of women globally is breast cancer. While there are no surefire ways to prevent breast cancer, upholding a healthy diet and way of living can help lower the likelihood of getting the disease. For those who have already been diagnosed with breast cancer, eating a healthy, balanced diet that contains all the nutrients they need can support their therapy and recovery.

the following essential nutrients and how they can be used to treat and avoid breast cancer:

Fiber: For healthy bowels and metabolism, fiber is crucial. It lowers the chance of developing colorectal cancer and aids in maintaining a regular digestive system. Additionally, fiber lowers blood sugar and lipid levels, two factors that can hasten the onset of breast cancer. Fruits, veggies, whole grains, nuts, and seeds are good sources of fiber.

Vitamins: The body requires a small amount of vitamins in order to operate properly. Vitamin D, for example, has been related to a lower chance of breast cancer. For the wellness of your bones and to help the body absorb calcium, take vitamin D. By controlling cell development and differentiation, it might also contribute to the prevention of breast cancer. Additionally crucial for immunological health and possibly preventing breast cancer are vitamins A, C, and E. Vegetables, fruits, dairy products, and whole grains are all excellent providers of vitamins.

Minerals: Minerals are necessary for a variety of bodily processes, such as the generation of energy, the immune system, and healthy bones. Particularly crucial for both preventing and treating breast cancer are the minerals calcium, magnesium, and zinc. Calcium supports healthy bones and may lower the chance of breast cancer. Magnesium is necessary for the production of energy and, by controlling estrogen levels, may help lower the chance of breast cancer. Zinc is crucial for immune system health and may lower the risk of breast cancer by slowing the development of tumors. Dairy products, lean meats, whole grains, nuts, and seeds are excellent providers of minerals.

Omega-3 fatty acids: The body requires omega-3 fatty acids as necessary fats for cognitive function, heart health, and inflammation control. According to some studies, omega-3 fatty acids may lessen inflammation and stop tumor growth in order to avoid breast cancer. Avocado, nuts, seeds, and fatty seafood are excellent sources of omega-3s.

Phytochemicals are naturally occurring substances that are found in plants and have anti-inflammatory and antioxidant qualities. There is evidence that some phytochemicals, including polyphenols, may lower the chance of breast cancer. Spices, whole grains, fruits, and veggies are excellent sources of phytochemicals.

Keeping up a nutritious diet can help lower the chance of developing breast cancer and support treatment and recovery for those who have already been diagnosed with the disease. Create a specialized nutrition plan that suits your particular requirements in collaboration with your nutritionist. A balanced diet rich in fiber, omega-3 fatty acids, vitamins, minerals, phytochemicals, and fiber can support immune function, lessen inflammation, and inhibit tumor development, eventually improving outcomes for those with breast cancer.

THE BODY NEEDS NUTRIENTS FOR NORMAL GROWTH AND FUNCTION

The body requires nutrients for proper growth and function. Nutrients are vital substances. These elements include fiber, good fats, vitamins, and minerals, as well as protein.

Protein: Protein is a crucial nutrient for the development and maintenance of bodily tissues. In addition, it is crucial for the body's ability to produce the hormones, enzymes, and other essential compounds. Meat, seafood, poultry, eggs, dairy products, beans, and nuts are all excellent sources of protein. Protein should be eaten in moderation because too much of it can have harmful effects on health.

Fiber is a form of carbohydrate that the body is unable to digest. In addition to preserving bowel health and regularity, it is crucial for lowering the chance of heart disease, diabetes, and some cancers. Fruits, veggies, whole grains, beans, and nuts are healthy forms of fiber. Adults should take in at least 25 to 30 grams of fiber daily.

Healthy Fats: Monounsaturated and polyunsaturated fats, in particular, are crucial for keeping hormone balance, heart health, and cognitive function. Healthy fats can be found in fatty seafood, nuts, seeds, avocados, and olive oil, among other foods. Trans and saturated fats should be eaten in moderation as they can have detrimental effects on health.

Vitamins: The body requires trace quantities of vitamins for healthy development and operation. They are crucial for keeping healthy skin, strong bones, and an effective immune system. Fruits, veggies, dairy products, and fortified cereals are excellent sources of vitamins. To ensure that all required vitamins are consumed, it is crucial to eat a variety of foods.

Minerals: The body requires minerals as important nutrients for healthy growth and operation. They are crucial for keeping healthy skin, strong bones, and an effective immune system. Dairy products, lean meats, whole grains, nuts, and seeds are excellent providers of minerals. To ensure that all required minerals are consumed, it is crucial to eat a variety of foods.

For optimum health, it's critical to consume a food rich in different nutrients. Healthy fats are important for maintaining heart health and cognitive function, fiber is important for maintaining bowel health and lowering the risk of disease, vitamins are essential for maintaining strong bones, healthy skin, and an efficient immune system, and nutrients are important for sustaining strong bones, healthy skin, and a strong immune system. Protein is essential for growth and repair. For optimum health, a balanced diet that consists of a range of foods from all food groups is advised.

RECOMMENDED DAILY INTAKE AND FOOD SOURCES FOR EACH NUTRIENT

Here is a summary of each nutrient's suggested daily intake as well as food sources:

Protein: Depending on factors like age, gender, weight, and degree of activity, different daily protein intakes are advised. Adults should generally ingest 0.8 grams of protein for every kilogram of body weight each day. Meats like beef, pig, lamb, veal, and game, poultry like chicken, turkey, and duck, and fish like salmon, tuna, mackerel, shrimp, and crab are all excellent sources of protein.

Chicken, pheasant, and duck eggs

Milk, cheese, yogurt, and cottage cheese are dairy products.

Beans, lentils, chickpeas, and peas are examples of legumes. Almonds, cashews, walnuts, pistachios, chia seeds, and flaxseeds are examples of nuts and seeds.

Fiber: For women, a daily intake of 25 grams of fiber is advised; for males, it is 38 grams. Fruits and vegetables such as apples, bananas, berries, oranges, and pears as well as broccoli, carrots, spinach, sweet potatoes, and tomatoes are excellent forms of fiber.

Legumes include lentils, black beans, kidney beans, and chickpeas. Whole grains include brown rice, quinoa, oats, and whole wheat bread. Nuts and seeds include walnuts, flaxseeds, chia seeds, and pumpkin seeds.

Healthy Fats: Depending on your age, gender, weight, and degree of activity, different healthy fats have different recommended daily intakes. Adults should generally ingest 20–35% of their daily calories from fat. Among the best sources of healthful fats are:

fatty seafood include sardines, tuna, mackerel, and salmon.

Almonds, pecans, flaxseeds, and chia seeds are among the nuts and seeds.

Avocado

Almond oil

Cocoa butter

Almond spread

Vitamins: Depending on your age, gender, and other variables, a daily vitamin intake is advised. Following are some typical vitamins and healthy dietary sources:

Sweet potatoes, beets, spinach, kale, and eggs all contain vitamin A.

Citrus vegetables, strawberries, kiwis, broccoli, and bell peppers all contain vitamin C.

fatty seafood, fortified milk, and fortified cereal all contain vitamin D.

Almonds, sunflower seeds, avocados, and greens all contain vitamin E.

Spinach, kale, collard vegetables, and broccoli all contain vitamin K.

Minerals: Depending on your age, gender, and other variables, different minerals have different daily intake recommendations. Following are some typical minerals and healthy dietary sources:

Dairy products, leafy green veggies, tofu, and cereal with added calcium

Meat, poultry, seafood, beans, lentils, and cereal with added iron

Spinach, almonds, avocados, and black legumes all contain magnesium.

Bananas, sweet potatoes, white legumes, and spinach all contain potassium.

Zinc foods include oysters, beef, pig, and fortified cereal.

CHAPTER 3

DIETARY RECOMMENDATIONS FOR

BREAST CANCER

A healthy diet is a crucial part of a treatment plan for breast cancer because it can help lower the chance of recurrence and enhance general health. Here are some basic breast cancer nutrition recommendations:

Consume a range of foods: The nutrients required for good health can be obtained from a diverse diet that includes fruits, veggies, whole grains, lean proteins, and healthy fats.

Put a priority on plant-based foods: Numerous health advantages of eating a diet high in plants have been demonstrated. As the base of your meals, choose fruits, veggies, whole grains, and legumes.

Keep processed and high-fat meals to a minimum: Processed foods, foods high in fat, and sugary beverages should all be avoided because they can increase inflammation and weight gain.

Pick lean proteins: Lean proteins, like those found in poultry, fish, turkey, beans, and lentils, can aid in tissue synthesis and repair as well as immune system support.

Pick healthy fats: Healthy fats can provide the important fatty acids required for good health, such as those found in avocados, nuts, seeds, and olive oil.

Stay away from alcohol: Drinking alcohol has been associated with a higher chance of breast cancer recurrence. Limit or stay away from drinking.

Choose low-glycemic index meals: Whole grains and non-starchy vegetables are examples of foods that can help control blood sugar levels.

Maintain adequate hydration levels by drinking plenty of water to help the body rid itself of toxins.

Think about supplements: Omega-3 fatty acids and vitamin D are two products that may be advantageous for people with breast cancer. Ask your doctor about any substances that might be suitable for you.

A healthy weight should be maintained because being overweight or obese increases the chance of breast cancer return. To reach and keep a healthy weight, consult a medical professional or certified dietitian.

Consume foods high in antioxidants because they may help shield cells from harm brought on by free radicals. Antioxidants include vitamins C and E. Berries, dark leafy vegetables, nuts, and seeds are foods high in antioxidants.

Include probiotics: Probiotics are good bacteria that can promote immune function and gut health. Probiotics are found in foods like yogurt, kefir, kimchi, and cabbage.

Limit your intake of red meat and processed meats: Consuming too much of these meats has been associated with an increased chance of developing certain cancers. Limit your intake of meat and choose leaner cuts.

Select dairy products with low fat content because some studies have linked consuming high fat dairy products to an increased chance of breast cancer. Instead, opt for low-fat dairy goods like skim milk and low-fat yogurt.

Food safety should be taken into consideration. Safe food handling and storage can help avoid foodborne illness, which can be especially harmful for people with compromised immune systems. Cook meals at the proper temperature, and wash your hands and surfaces frequently.

Take into account any nutritional requirements: Breast cancer therapy can result in side effects like nausea, diarrhea, and mouth sores, which can make eating challenging. Consult a trained dietitian or a healthcare professional for advice on how to use diet to manage these side effects.

Avoid fad diets: Fad diets, such as those that guarantee rapid weight reduction or eliminate entire food groups, are typically neither healthy nor sustainable. Put your energy into changing your diet and way of living gradually and sustainably.

RECOMMENDED FOODS FOR PATIENTS WITH BREAST CANCER

The secret to a breast cancer diet is to choose nutrient-rich, whole foods. Here are some foods for breast cancer sufferers who are just starting out:

Vegetables and fruits: Vegetables and fruits are abundant in vitamins, minerals, fiber, and phytonutrients. Incorporate as many different hues of berries, leafy veggies, broccoli, carrots, and sweet potatoes into your diet as you can.

Whole grains: Whole grains are a valuable source of fiber and additional minerals like iron and B vitamins. Pick brown rice, quinoa, and barley as well as whole grain bread, noodles, and cereal.

Lean proteins can support the immune system and encourage tissue repair. Examples of lean proteins include poultry, turkey, fish, beans, lentils, and tofu.

Essential fatty acids can be provided by healthy fats, which are, for example, those found in almonds, seeds, avocados, and olive oil. These fats can also help to lessen inflammation.

Low-fat dairy products are an excellent source of calcium and other vital nutrients. Examples include skim milk and low-fat yogurt.

Foods high in probiotics: Foods high in probiotics, such as yogurt, kefir, kimchi, and sauerkraut, can strengthen the immune system and gut health.

Herbs and spices: Spices and herbs like rosemary, ginger, garlic, and curcumin may have anti-inflammatory properties.

Water: It's critical to maintain hydration for general health and wellbeing. Make an effort to hydrate yourself well throughout the day.

Cruciferous vegetables: Cruciferous vegetables, including kale, broccoli, and cauliflower, contain substances that may have anti-cancer qualities.

Berry: Antioxidant-rich berries, like blueberries and strawberries, may have anti-inflammatory and other health advantages.

Green tea: Catechins, which are found in green tea, may have anti-cancer effects.

Foods made from soy: Isoflavones, which are present in soy products like tofu and soybeans, may have anti-cancer effects.

Omega-3 fatty acids: Flaxseed, walnuts, salmon, and other fatty fish are rich sources of omega-3 fatty acids, which may have anti-inflammatory and other health advantages.

It's crucial to remember that while some foods may have particular advantages for people who have breast cancer, there isn't a single "magic" food or nutrient that can stop or heal the disease. Overall health and wellbeing can be supported by eating a diverse, balanced diet that prioritizes whole, nutrient-dense foods.

Foods To Avoid

There are some foods that people with breast cancer may want to limit or avoid, even though no specific food or food group has been demonstrated to cause or cure the disease. A beginner with breast cancer should stay away from the items listed below:

Meat that has been processed: Meat that has been processed includes bacon, sausage, and hot dogs. These meats have high sodium and nitrate content, which has been associated with an increased chance of certain cancers.

Dairy products high in fat: Some studies have found a connection between eating dairy products high in fat and having a higher chance of breast cancer. Instead, opt for low-fat dairy goods like skim milk and low-fat yogurt.

Beverages with added sugar: Sugar-sweetened drinks, like soda and sports drinks, can cause weight gain and inflammation, both of which raise the chance of developing certain cancers.

Alcohol: Drinking alcohol has been associated with a higher chance of breast cancer. If you choose to consume booze, do so sparingly. (no more than one drink per day for women).

Foods that have been fried or charred: Cooking meat at high temperatures, such as grilling or frying, can result in the production of dangerous chemicals called heterocyclic amines (HCAs) and polycyclic aromatic hydrocarbons (PAHs), which have been related to an increased chance of certain cancers.

Refined carbs: Refined carbs, like white bread, white rice, and sugary snacks, can cause weight gain and inflammation, which may raise the chance of developing some cancers.

Trans fats: Trans fats, which are present in processed foods like margarine and baked goods, have been connected to a higher chance of developing some types of cancer.

PORTION SIZES AND MEAL ROUTINE

Managing your diet and nutrition can be crucial to your therapy and recovery as a new breast cancer patient. The frequency of meals and portion sizes are two aspects of healthful eating that are frequently disregarded. Knowing when to consume and how much to eat can help you avoid overfeeding your body with unhealthy foods or excess calories while still giving it the nutrients it needs.

Meal frequency refers to how frequently you eat throughout the day, whereas portion sizes allude to how much food you eat at one sitting. Here are some pointers for controlling dinner frequency and portion sizes as a new breast cancer patient:

Utilize a graphic aid: Utilizing a visual aid, such as the plate technique, is one way to gauge portion sizes. Four parts should be on your plate: one for protein, one for starchy vegetables or whole grains, and two for non-starchy vegetables or fruit. This can ensure that you are not overeating and are receiving a balanced mix of nutrients.

Pay attention to serving sizes: Monitoring the serving sizes stated on nutrition labels is a further strategy for controlling portion sizes. It may be simpler to regulate portion sizes because many foods are available in pre-packaged portions. To measure out foods like grains, nuts, and seeds, you can also use measuring cups and spoons.

It's crucial to pay attention to your body's signals of appetite and fullness. When you're hungry, eat, and when you're full, cease. This can assist in lowering the chance of certain cancers by preventing overeating and weight gain.

Eat modest, frequent meals throughout the day to help control blood sugar levels and avoid overindulging. Try to consume at regular intervals and aim for three meals and two to three snacks per day.

Avoid skipping meals because doing so can lower blood sugar levels, which can result in overeating and weight increase. Additionally, it may hinder your body's ability to recover from the side effects of cancer therapy. Even if they are small meals, try to consume three meals a day.

Pick nutrient-rich foods: Eat foods that are rich in vitamins, minerals, and other healthy compounds that are nutrient-dense. Fruits, veggies, whole grains, lean proteins, and healthy fats can all fall under this category.

Limit processed foods: Processed foods can be high in calories, bad fats, and added sugars. Examples include packaged munchies, fast food, and sugary beverages. Limiting these foods will help you concentrate more on whole, nutrient-dense foods.

You can support your body's health and healing as a breast cancer new patient by controlling your portion sizes and meal frequency. Always pay attention to your body's signals, select foods that are high in nutrients, and collaborate with a healthcare professional or certified dietitian to create a personalized nutrition plan that takes into account your unique requirements and medical background.

CHAPTER 4

RECIPES FOR BREAKFAST

Eating a nutritious breakfast every day is crucial if you're a breast cancer beginner patient. A healthy breakfast can help control blood sugar levels, increase energy, and give your body the nutrients it needs to promote recovery and healing. Here are some tasty and healthy breakfast dishes for people with cancer:

Oats overnight: Because they can be made the night before and kept in the refrigerator, overnight oats are a fantastic choice for hectic mornings. Simply mix milk or yogurt, rolled oats, and your preferred fruit, nut, and seed combinations in a jar or bowl. Enjoy the combination in the morning after letting it chill in the fridge all night. You can add different tastes to overnight oats, like peanut butter and banana or apple cinnamon.

Smoothies: Smoothies can be a nutrient-dense breakfast choice that is quick and simple. Combine a variety of fruits, veggies, and protein sources with a liquid base like milk or almond milk, such as Greek yogurt or tofu. A fruit spinach smoothie or a tropical green smoothie are two delectable smoothie concoctions.

Avocado toast: Avocado toast is a trendy, delectable, and healthful breakfast choice. Toasted whole grain bread should only be topped with pureed avocado, tomato slices, salt, and pepper. Add a poached or cooked egg on top for more protein.

Greek yogurt parfait: Greek yogurt, which is a fantastic source of calcium and protein, tastes excellent when combined with your favorite fruits, nuts, and seeds. For a filling meal, layer Greek yogurt, fresh fruit, and granola or chopped nuts in a container or bowl.

Egg muffin cups are a customizable breakfast choice that can be made ahead of time using your preferred vegetables and protein sources. Eggs, milk, chopped veggies like spinach, bell peppers, and mushrooms, cooked meat like chicken or turkey, and all of these ingredients should be whisked together. Fill a muffin pan with the batter, and bake it there until done. You can keep these egg muffin cups in the freezer or fridge for a quick and simple breakfast alternative.

As a breast cancer new patient, it's crucial to concentrate on nutrient-dense foods that offer a mix of carbohydrates, protein, and healthy fats for breakfast. These breakfast ideas for cancer patients offer a selection of delectable and wholesome choices that can be altered to suit your particular dietary requirements and taste preferences.

Several breakfast dishes are available, such as smoothies, oatmeal, eggs, and breakfast wraps.

Here are a few easy-to-make, wholesome, and delectable breakfast dishes for breast cancer patients:

Ingredients for Breakfast Recipe No. 1's Berry Banana Smoothie

one big banana

One-half cup of frozen mixed fruit

Greek yogurt, half a cup

12 cup coconut milk without sugar

1 tablespoon of honey (optional)

Instructions

In a blender, combine all the components and process until completely smooth.

If necessary, add more water or almond milk to achieve the desired viscosity.

Enjoy the smoothie by pouring it into a tumbler.

5 minutes to prepare

Ingredients for Breakfast Recipe #2's Creamy Oatmeal

Oats, folded, in a cup

one water cup

12 cup coconut milk without sugar

1 tablespoon of honey (optional)

12 teaspoon cinnamon

1/2 cup of chopped fruit or nuts

Instructions

• In a medium saucepan, combine the dried oats, water, and almond milk. Bring to a boil.

• Lower the heat, cover, and simmer the mixture for 10 to 12 minutes, stirring periodically, until the oats are tender and the mixture is creamy.

• Add honey and cinnamon, and then sprinkle berries or other diced fruit on top.

15 minutes for preparation

Eggs scrambled with spinach and feta are the third breakfast recipe.

two huge embryos

one cup of new greens

1/4 cup feta cheese crumbles

1 teaspoon olive oil

pepper and salt as desired

Instructions

• Beat the eggs with salt and pepper in a small dish.

• In a small nonstick pan over medium-high heat, warm the olive oil.

• Add the greens and cook until wilted for 2–3 minutes.

• Add the beaten eggs to the pan and cook them until set, stirring periodically.

• Sprinkle feta cheese crumbles on top and serve.

10 minutes for preparation

Ingredients for Breakfast Recipe No. 4's Breakfast Wrap

1 tortilla whole-wheat

2 big scrambled eggs

50 ml of black legumes

14 cup of tomatoes, diced

1-fourth cup of sliced avocado

1/4 cup of cheddar cheese, sliced

pepper and salt as desired

Instructions

• In a dry pan over medium heat, warm the tortilla for 30 seconds on each side.

On top of the tortilla, arrange the scrambled eggs, black beans, tomatoes, guacamole, and cheddar cheese.

• Fold the tortilla's edges toward the center, then roll it up firmly.

• Cut into halves and serve.

15 minutes for preparation

CHAPTER 5

RECIPES FOR LUNCH AND DINNER

Here are some tasty and healthy cancer diet lunch and supper recipes:

Recipe #1

Skewers of grilled chicken and vegetables

Ingredients

2 skinless, boneless breasts of poultry

one scarlet bell pepper, chopped

one golden bell pepper, chopped

Sliced zucchini from 1

one scarlet onion, chopped

2/TBS of olive oil

2 chopped garlic cloves

Dry oregano, 1 teaspoon

pepper and salt as desired

Instructions

- Heat the griddle to a medium-high setting.

- Slice the poultry into bite-sized pieces and alternate the vegetables and chicken on skewers.

- Combine olive oil, garlic, thyme, salt, and pepper in a small dish.

When the poultry is cooked through and the vegetables are tender, brush the skewers with the oil mixture and grill for 10 to 12 minutes, turning once or twice.

20 minutes for preparation

Recipe #2

Quinoa and Veggie Stir-Fry,

Ingredients

1 cup rinsed rice

2-cups of water

1 tablespoon of olive oil

Chopped red scallion, one

1 chopped scarlet bell pepper

2 chopped garlic cloves

broccoli stems in a cup

Sliced mushrooms in a cup

Low-sodium soy sauce, 14 cup

1 tablespoon of honey

Grated ginger, 1 teaspoon

1 teaspoon powder

pepper and salt as desired

Instructions

Quinoa and water should be combined in a medium pot and brought to a boil.

• Lower the heat to a medium setting, cover the pan, and simmer the quinoa for 15 to 20 minutes, or until the water has been absorbed.

Olive oil should be heated to a medium-high temperature in a big pan.

• Add the broccoli, mushrooms, onion, bell pepper, garlic, and sauté for 5 to 7 minutes, or until the veggies are tender.

• Combine soy sauce, honey, ginger, cornstarch, salt, and pepper in a small dish.

Vegetables should be covered with sauce after being poured over them and stirred.

Stir the cooked quinoa into the mixture after adding it to the pan.

30 minutes for preparation

Salmon Baked with Roasted Vegetables, Recipe #3

Ingredients

4 salmon pieces, 4 ounces

a pound of mixed veggies (e.g. carrots, zucchini, asparagus, tomatoes)

2/TBS of olive oil

2 chopped garlic cloves

Dried oregano, 1 teaspoon

pepper and salt as desired

Instructions

• Set the oven to 400 °F.

• Use parchment paper to line a baking tray.

The salmon fillets should be arranged on the baking tray.

• Combine olive oil, garlic, oregano, salt, and pepper in a small dish.

Salmon fillets should be brushed with the oil combination.

• Arrange the assorted veggies around the salmon fillets on the baking sheet.

• Apply the leftover oil mixture to the vegetables with a brush.

• Bake for 15-20 minutes, or until the veggies are soft and the salmon is thoroughly cooked.

30 minutes for preparation

Ingredients for

Recipe #4

Lentil and Vegetable Soup

1 cup rinsed dried green or brown legumes

4 cups of veggie broth low in sodium

one sliced onion

2 chopped garlic cloves

2 sliced carrots

2 chopped celery stems

1 undrained can of chopped tomatoes

Dry oregano, 1 teaspoon

1 teaspoon dried oregano

pepper and salt as desired

garnishing with fresh cilantro (optional)

Instructions

• Place lentils, veggie broth, onion, celery, carrots, tomatoes, thyme, rosemary, salt, and pepper in a large pot.

• Bring to a boil, lower the heat, cover, and simmer for 30 to 40 minutes, depending on how tender you like your legumes.

• If preferred, top with fresh parsley when serving.

15 minutes for preparation, 40 minutes for cooking

Recipe #5

Stir-fried brown rice and vegetables

Ingredients

1 cup drained brown rice

2-cups of water

1 tablespoon of olive oil

Chopped red scallion, one

1 sliced red bell pepper 2 minced garlic cloves

broccoli stems in a cup

Sliced mushrooms in a cup

Low-sodium soy sauce, 14 cup

1 tablespoon of honey

Grated ginger, 1 teaspoon

1 teaspoon powder

pepper and salt as desired

Instructions

• Place brown rice and water in a medium saucepan and come to a boil.

• Lower the heat to a medium setting, cover the pot, and simmer the rice for 35 to 40 minutes, or until the water has been absorbed.

Olive oil should be heated to a medium-high temperature in a big pan.

• Add the broccoli, mushrooms, onion, bell pepper, garlic, and sauté for 5 to 7 minutes, or until the veggies are tender.

• Combine soy sauce, honey, ginger, cornstarch, salt, and pepper in a small dish.

Vegetables should be covered with sauce after being poured over them and stirred.

Stir the brown rice to incorporate after adding it to the skillet.

30 minutes for preparation

Recipe #6

Stir-fried chicken and vegetables

Ingredients

2 chicken breasts, cut into bite-sized chunks, are boneless and skinless.

2/TBS of olive oil

Chopped red scallion, one

1 chopped scarlet bell pepper

2 chopped garlic cloves

broccoli stems in a cup

Sliced mushrooms in a cup

Low-sodium soy sauce, 14 cup

1 tablespoon of honey

Grated ginger, 1 teaspoon

1 teaspoon powder

pepper and salt as desired

Instructions

Olive oil should be heated to a medium-high temperature in a big pan.

• Add the chicken and sauté it for 5-7 minutes, or until it is thoroughly cooked and browned.

• Take the chicken out of the pan and place it away.

• To the skillet, add the broccoli, mushrooms, onion, bell pepper, garlic, and sauté for 5 to 7 minutes, or until the veggies are tender.

• Combine soy sauce, honey, ginger, cornstarch, salt, and pepper in a small dish.

Vegetables should be covered with sauce after being poured over them and stirred.

Stirring the contents together, add the cooked chicken back to the pan.

30 minutes for preparation

Quinoa and Roasted Vegetable Salad Ingredients from Recipe #7

1 cup rinsed rice

2-cups of water

2/TBS of olive oil

Chop one red onion, one red bell pepper, one zucchini, one yellow squash, and one cup cherry tomatoes.

Balsamic vinegar, 2 tbsp.

pepper and salt as desired

garnished with fresh mint (optional)

Instructions

• Set the oven temperature to 425°F (218°C).

• Quinoa and water should be combined and brought to a boil in a medium pot.

• Lower the heat to a medium setting, cover the pan, and simmer the quinoa for 15 to 20 minutes, or until the water has been absorbed.

• Combine zucchini, yellow squash, onion, bell pepper, and cherry tomatoes in a large dish. Drizzle with olive oil and season with salt and pepper.

• Arrange the veggies in a single layer on a baking sheet, and roast for 20 to 25 minutes, or until they are soft and lightly browned.

• Combine balsamic vinegar, salt, and pepper in a small dish.

• Toss the roasted veggies and cooked quinoa in the bowl with the balsamic dressing.

• Garnish with fresh basil, if preferred, and serve warm or chilled.

15 minutes for preparation, 25 minutes for cooking

Ingredients for Recipe #8's tuna salad with avocado and chickpeas

1 can (5 ounce) flaked and drained tuna

1 sliced and peeled avocado

1 can (15 oz) rinsed and drained beans

1 chopped scarlet bell pepper

14 cup finely minced red scallion

2/TBS of olive oil

1.5 tbsp citrus juice

pepper and salt as desired

garnishing with fresh cilantro (optional)

Instructions

• Combine the tuna, avocado, chickpeas, bell pepper, and onion in a big dish.

• Combine olive oil, lemon juice, salt, and pepper in a small dish.

• Drizzle the tuna combination with the dressing and toss to combine.

• If preferred, garnish with fresh parsley and serve chilled.

10 minutes for preparation

Recipe #9

Salmon and asparagus

Ingredients

2 pieces of salmon (6 oz each)

1 tablespoon of olive oil

1-tablespoon citrus juice

1 chopped garlic clove

pepper and salt as desired

1 cut bunch of asparagus

shredded Parmesan cheese, 1 tablespoon

Instructions

- Set the oven temperature to 375°F (190°C).

- Combine the olive oil, lemon juice, garlic, salt, and pepper in a small dish.

Salmon fillets should be placed in a baking tray and coated with the olive oil mixture.

- Place asparagus all around the salmon, then top with Parmesan.

- Bake the salmon and asparagus for 15-20 minutes, or until the salmon is cooked through.

- ten minutes to prepare, Cook for 15 to 20 minutes.

SALADS AND SOUPS

For a breast cancer patient who is just starting out, here are some nutritious and simple soup and salad recipes:

Recipe #10

Broccoli and Cheese Soup

Ingredients

1 stalk of chopped broccoli

one sliced onion

2 cups of veggie or chicken broth

1 cup cream or milk

1 cup of cheddar cheese, shredded

pepper and salt as desired

Instructions

• Cook the onion in olive oil in a big pot until it becomes translucent and soft.

Bring the broccoli, broth, and other ingredients to a boil.

• Lower the heat to low and let the broccoli simmer for 20 to 25 minutes, or until tender.

• Use an immersion blender or a blender to puree the soup until it is smooth.

• Add the grated cheese and milk or cream.

Add salt and pepper to taste when seasoning.

• Serve warm.

10 minutes for preparation, 30 minutes for cooking

Recipe #11

Salad of spinach and quinoa

Ingredients

1 cup rinsed rice

2-cups of water

3 cups of young spinach

1 chopped scarlet bell pepper

1 chopped avocado

14 cup finely minced red scallion

chopped walnuts, 1/4 cup

2/TBS of olive oil

1.5 tbsp citrus juice

pepper and salt as desired

Instructions

Quinoa and water should be combined in a medium pot and brought to a boil.

• Lower the heat to a medium setting, cover the pan, and simmer the quinoa for 15 to 20 minutes, or until the water has been absorbed.

• Combine the cooked quinoa, spinach, red bell pepper, avocado, red onion, and walnuts in a sizable bowl.

• Combine olive oil, lemon juice, salt, and pepper in a small dish.

• Drizzle the salad with the dressing and toss to combine.

• Offer chilled.

10 minutes for preparation, 20 minutes for cooking.

Ingredients for Recipe No. 12 for Tomato and Basil Soup

2/TBS of olive oil

one sliced onion

2 minced garlic cloves

three cups of diced tomatoes

2 cups of veggie or chicken broth

14 cup finely minced fresh basil

pepper and salt as desired

Instructions

- Heat the olive oil in a big pot over medium heat.

- Stir in the onion and garlic, cooking until fragrant.

Bring the broth to a boil before adding the chopped tomatoes.

- Lower the heat to low and simmer the tomatoes for 20 to 25 minutes, or until they are soft.

- Use an immersion blender or a blender to puree the soup until it is smooth.

- Add the chopped basil and stir.

Add salt and pepper to taste when seasoning.

- Serve warm.

10 minutes for preparation, 25 minutes for cooking

Recipe # 13

Salad with goat cheese and beets

Ingredients

3 cups of greens, mixed

2 cooked, chopped beets

1/2 cup goat cheese crumbles

chopped walnuts, 1/4 cup

2/TBS of olive oil

Balsamic vinegar, 2 tbsp.

pepper and salt as desired

Instructions

Combine mixed greens, diced beets, crumbled goat cheese, and chopped walnuts in a big bowl.

Mix the olive oil, balsamic vinegar, salt, and pepper in a small bowl.Pour the dressing over the salad and toss to coat.

Serve chilled.

Prep time: 10 minutes, Cook time: 0 minutes

Recipe #14

Lentil and Vegetable Soup

Ingredients

Red legumes, 1 cup

one sliced onion

2 minced garlic cloves

1 sliced carrot

1 diced celery stem

1 sliced zucchini

one tomato chopped in a can

4 cups of veggie broth low in sodium

Turmeric, 1 teaspoon

1 teaspoon of coriander seeds

To flavor, add salt and black pepper.

chopped fresh cilantro as a garnish

Instructions

Lentils should be rinsed in cold water and put aside.

• Soften the shallots and garlic in a big pot.

• Stir well after adding the chopped tomatoes, zucchini, celery, and carrots.

• Bring to a boil the lentils, veggie broth, turmeric, and cumin.

• Lower the heat, cover the pot, and simmer the lentils for 20 to 25 minutes, or until they are soft.

Add black pepper and salt to flavor.

• Garnish with fresh parsley and serve steaming.

Recipe #15

Ingredients in a kale and quinoa salad

quinoa cooked into two glasses

1 bunch of kale, with the stalks cut off and minced

1 sliced avocado

one grated carrot and one chopped red bell pepper

1 can of rinsed and drained beans

Pumpkin seeds, 2 tablespoons

Sunflower seeds, 2 tablespoons

Extra-virgin olive oil, 2 tablespoons

Balsamic vinegar, 1 tablespoon

To flavor, add salt and black pepper.

Instructions

• Combine cooked quinoa, kale, avocado, carrot, red bell pepper, and chickpeas in a sizable dish.

• Mix well after adding the pumpkin seeds and sunflower seeds.

• Combine olive oil and balsamic vinegar in a small dish.

• Drizzle the lettuce with the dressing and toss thoroughly.

Add black pepper and salt to flavor.

• Whenever possible, serve warm.

Recipe #16

Beet and Carrot Salad

Ingredients

Peeled and grated, two medium-sized carrots

2 peeled and shredded carrots

2 tbsp of freshly chopped cilantro

2 tablespoons of freshly cut mint

1/4 cup of feta cheese crumbles

Extra-virgin olive oil, 2 tablespoons

Lemon juice, one tablespoon

To flavor, add salt and black pepper.

Instructions

• Combine grated beets, grated carrots, chopped parsley, and chopped mint in a large dish.

• Stir in the feta cheese crumbles.

• Mix the lemon juice and olive oil in a small dish.

• After adding the vinaigrette, thoroughly toss the salad.

Add black pepper and salt to flavor.Offer.

CHAPTER 6

SNACK RECIPES

Healthy snack recipes that are suitable for a breast cancer beginner:

Recipe #1

Ingredients for Greek Yogurt with Berries

Greek yogurt, one cup

a half-cup of fruit. (blueberries, raspberries, and strawberries)

10 grams of honey

walnuts, cut into 1/4 cup

Instructions

• Combine Greek yogurt and honey in a dish.

Add mixed fruit and combine thoroughly.

• Add minced walnuts to the top.

• Offer chilled.

Recipe #2

Apple and Almond Butter Slices

Ingredients

1 chopped apple

Almond butter, two tablespoons.

Chia nuts, 1 tablespoon

Instructions

Apple pieces with almond butter on them.

Chia seeds should be added on top.

• Serve right away.

Recipe #3

Roasted Chickpeas

Ingredients

1 can of rinsed and drained beans

Extra-virgin olive oil, 1 tablespoon

1 teaspoon of coriander seeds

Smoked paprika, 1 teaspoon

Garlic powder, half a teaspoon

To flavor, add salt and black pepper.

Instructions

• Set the oven to 200°C (400°F).

• After rinsing them in cool water, pat dry the chickpeas.

• Combine chickpeas, cumin, smoked paprika, garlic powder, olive oil, salt, and black pepper in a dish.

On a baking pan, spread the chickpeas in a single layer.

• Roast until golden, about 20 to 25 minutes.

• Whether to serve it heated or cold.

Recipe #4

Hummus and carrot dip

Ingredients

2 peeled and sliced carrots

1/fourth cup of hummus

Lemon juice, one tablespoon

1 tablespoon freshly chopped cilantro

Instructions

• Steam carrots until they are tender.

• Blend hummus, steamed carrots, lemon juice, and cilantro until completely smooth.

• Serve chilled with raw veggies like bell pepper, celery, and cucumber.

Ingredients for Recipe #5 for Baked Sweet Potato Chips

2 pieces of thinly sliced sweet potatoes

Extra-virgin olive oil, 1 tablespoon

Sea salt, 1/2 teaspoon

Black pepper, 1/4 teaspoon

Oven should be preheated to 400°F (200°C).

Sweet potato slices, olive oil, sea salt, and black pepper should all be combined in a dish.

• Arrange sweet potato pieces on a baking sheet in a single layer.

• Bake until golden, about 15 to 20 minutes.

• Whether to serve it heated or cold.

Recipe #6

Berry Smoothie

Ingredients

one cup of frozen mixed fruit (blueberries, raspberries, and strawberries)

Greek yogurt basic, half a cup

Almond milk, half a cup

Honey, 1/2 tsp.

Vanilla essence, 1/4 teaspoon

Instructions • Blend the Greek yogurt, almond milk, honey, and vanilla essence with the mixed berries.

Blend until emulsified.

Pour cold liquid into a glass and serve.

Recipe #7

Tuna Salad

Ingredients

1 can of drained mackerel

Greek yogurt, basic, one-fourth cup

14 cup of celery, sliced

Red onion, sliced into 1/4 cup

1 tablespoon freshly sliced dill

Lemon juice, one teaspoon

To flavor, add salt and black pepper.

Instructions

Tuna, Greek yogurt, celery, red onion, dill, lemon juice, salt, and black pepper should all be combined in a dish.

• Place the dish on top of a bed of mixed vegetables or alongside whole-grain crackers.

Ingredients for Recipe No. 8: Roasted Nuts

1 cup of uncooked, mixed nuts (almonds, walnuts, pecans, and cashews)

Extra-virgin olive oil, 1 tablespoon

powdered rosemary, 1 teaspoon

Garlic powder, half a teaspoon

To flavor, add salt and black pepper.

Instructions

• Set the oven to 350 °F (or 175 °C).

• Combine raw nuts, olive oil, rosemary that has been dried, garlic powder, salt, and black pepper in a dish.

• Arrange nuts on a baking tray in a single layer.

• Roast for 10 to 15 minutes, or until aromatic and just beginning to brown.

• Whether to serve it heated or cold.

These quick and simple snack recipes can be prepared at any moment of the day. They are all nutrient-dense, high in fiber, packed with good fats, and full of antioxidants, which can offer a breast cancer sufferer a number of health advantages.

CHAPTER 7

DESSERT RECIPES

Some breast cancer-friendly dessert recipes that are easy to make and delicious:

Recipe #1

Berry Chia Seed Pudding

Ingredients

Chia seeds, 1/4 cup

1 cup of coconut milk without sugar

1/2 cup of fresh fruit, mixed. (blueberries, raspberries, and strawberries)

Honey, 1 teaspoon (optional)

Vanilla essence, 1/4 teaspoon

Instructions

Chia seeds, almond milk, honey (if using), and vanilla essence should all be combined in a bowl.

• Give the combination a thorough stir and allow to cool for at least 30 minutes, or until the mixture thickens.

Chia seed pudding and mixed berries should be layered in a serving container or jar and served cold.

recipe #2

Apples baked with cinnamon and almonds (

Ingredients

2 cored and cut apples

Almonds, minced, 2 tablespoons

10 grams of honey

1/2 teaspoon of cinnamon, powdered

Nutmeg, 1/4 teaspoon

Butter, unadulterated, 1 tablespoon

Instructions

• Set oven temperature to 375°F (190°C).

• Combine sliced apples, chopped almonds, honey, cinnamon powder, and nutmeg in a dish.

•   The apple combination should be placed into a baking dish that has been greased with unsalted butter.

• Bake the apples for 20 to 25 minutes, or until they are tender and just starting to color.

• Whether to serve it heated or cold.

Recipe #3

Ingredients

Chocolate Avocado Pudding

Two mature bananas

Unsweetened chocolate powder, 1/4 cup

unadulterated maple syrup in a quarter cup

1/4 cup of coconut milk without sugar

Vanilla essence, 1 teaspoon

a dash of salt, the water

• Blend avocado, cocoa powder, maple syrup, almond milk, vanilla essence, and sea salt in a blender.

Blend until buttery and smooth.

• Ladle the pudding into small bowls for serving.

• Chill in the refrigerator for at least an hour.

Serve chilled.

Recipe #4

Greek Yogurt and Fruit Parfait

Ingredients 1 cup of unsweetened Greek yogurt

1/2 cup of fresh berry mixture (blueberries, raspberries, and strawberries)

Granola, 1/4 cup

Honey, 1 teaspoon (optional)

Instructions Layer Greek yogurt, mixed fruits, granola, and honey in a serving container or jar. (if using).

• Continue layering the glass or jar until it is filled.

• Offer chilled.

Recipe #5

Banana Almond Butter Bites

Ingredients

two ripe mangoes

Almond butter, two tablespoons.

1/4 cup of coconut shavings without sugar

1/4 cup of nuts, chopped

Instructions

Bananas should be cut into bite-sized chunks.

• Cover each piece of banana with almond butter.

• Coat the banana segments with chopped almonds and coconut flakes.

• Arrange the bite-sized pieces of banana almond butter on a baking tray covered with parchment paper.

• Freeze for a couple of hours, or until solid.

• Offer chilled.

Recipe #6

Ingredients

Peanut Butter Chocolate Protein Balls

Rolling oats in a cup

peanut butter, half a cup

unadulterated maple syrup in a quarter cup

Unsweetened chocolate powder, 1/4 cup

Vanilla protein powder, 1/4 cup

a dash of salt, the water

Instructions

• Pulverize dried oats into a fine powder in a food processor.

Sea salt, protein powder, chocolate powder, maple syrup, and peanut butter can all be added. until everything is thoroughly mixed, pulse.

• Make little balls out of the dough.

• Arrange the protein balls with peanut butter and chocolate on a baking tray covered with parchment paper.

• Place in the fridge for at least an hour, or until solid.

• Offer chilled.

Recipe #7

Pears Baked with Walnuts and Honey,

Ingredients

Sliced and cored two apples

walnuts, cut into 1/4 cup

Honey, 2 tablespoons

1/2 teaspoon of cinnamon, powdered

1/8 teaspoon of ginger powder

Instructions

- Preheat oven to 375°F (190°C).

- In a bowl, mix sliced pears, chopped walnuts, honey, ground cinnamon, and ground ginger.

- Grease a baking dish with unsalted butter and add the pear mixture to the dish.

- Bake for 20-25 minutes or until the pears are soft and lightly browned.

- Serve hot or at room temperature.

DESSERTS RECIPES THAT ARE HIGH IN NUTRIENTS AND LOW IN SUGAR

Desserts for people newly diagnosed with breast cancer should focus on being high in nutrition and low in sugar. In addition to supplying the body with necessary nutrients to support general health and wellbeing, this aids in maintaining a healthy blood sugar level. Here are some appropriate treat choices:

Produce Salad

A excellent dessert option that is naturally low in sugar and high in nutrients is a fruit salad. Your preferred fruits, like strawberries, raspberries, kiwis, mangoes, and pineapple, can be combined. For additional creaminess and flavor, you can also drizzle honey or add a dollop of Greek yogurt to the fruit salad's top.

The Chia Pudding

A wonderful treat choice that is high in fiber, protein, and omega-3 fatty acids is chia pudding. Additionally, it is inherently low in sugar and is simple to alter to your personal tastes. Chia seeds, unsweetened almond milk, vanilla extract, and a natural sweetener like pure maple syrup or honey should be combined to create chia pudding. Allow the combination to chill in the refrigerator for at least two hours or overnight, or until it thickens and resembles pudding. For more taste and crunch, you can also add toppings like finely chopped nuts or fresh berries.

Boiling Apples

An excellent dessert choice that is low in sugar and inherently sweet is baked apples. Slice and core the apples, then put them in a baking dish to create baked apples. Add cinnamon and a natural sweetener, such as unadulterated maple syrup or honey, to the apples. The apples should be soft and golden colored after about 20 minutes of baking at 375°F (190°C). Additionally, you can add some chopped pecans or a dollop of Greek yogurt to the baked apples as a garnish.

Dark Chocolate

The health benefits of dark chocolate, which is high in antioxidants and a delicious dessert choice, have been demonstrated to include reducing inflammation and enhancing heart health. For a sweet indulgence after meals, choose dark chocolate that contains at least 70% cocoa.

Parfait of Greek yogurt

Greek yogurt is a fantastic source of calcium and protein, and it makes a delectable and nutritious dessert when mixed with fresh fruit and nuts. Greek yogurt, fresh berries, and chopped nuts should all be layered in a glass or dish to create a parfait. For even more sweetness, drizzle with unadulterated maple syrup or honey.

All of these treats are low in sugar and high in nutrients, making them excellent choices for people newly diagnosed with breast cancer. They are simple to prepare and can be eaten as a sweet treat without compromising your nutritional or health objectives.

CHAPTER 8

MEAL PLANNING

Assuring that patients are consuming the proper nutrients to support their general health and well-being is a key component of managing breast cancer. Additionally, it can assist in controlling treatment-related adverse effects like nausea, exhaustion, and appetite loss. Here are some pointers for developing a wholesome and balanced diet plan for those new to breast cancer:

Seek Advice From A Registered Dietitian

You can get assistance from a registered dietitian in developing a customized meal plan based on your unique requirements and tastes. Additionally, they can assist you in controlling any treatment-related adverse effects and guarantee that you are consuming the proper nutrients to support your general health and wellbeing.

Specify a Range of Foods

All of the food groups, including fruits, veggies, whole grains, lean proteins, and healthy fats, should be represented in a nutritious meal plan. This guarantees that you are consuming all the necessary nutrients for your body's correct operation.

Put Whole Foods First

Whole foods are those that have undergone minimum processing and contain little to no artificial sweeteners, salts, or flavors. Fruits, veggies, whole grains, lean proteins, nuts, and seeds are a few examples of whole foods. These foods are full of antioxidants, vitamins, and minerals, which can promote general health and wellbeing.

Make Ahead Plans For Meals And Snacks

Planning your meals and snacks in preparation can ensure that you always have wholesome options on hand. When you lack time or energy, this can also help you avoid overeating or making unhealthy food decisions.

Think about meal preparation

Preparing meals and refreshments ahead of time ensures they are available for consumption throughout the workweek. By doing this, you can save time and effort and make sure that you always have wholesome food on hand.

For Flavor, Use Herbs And Spices

Spices and herbs are excellent ways to flavor food without adding additional fat or sodium. Additionally, they have antioxidant and anti-inflammatory properties, which can promote general health and wellbeing.

Keep Hydrated

Staying hydrated is crucial for general health and can help with treatment-related side effects like nausea and fatigue. At least 8 to 10 cups of water should be consumed each day. You should also think about including hydrating foods like fruits and veggies in your diet.

A Few Ideas for Ahead-of-Time Meal and Snack Planning

For people newly diagnosed with breast cancer, making meal and snack plans in advance is a good way to stay on task with their diet and make sure they are getting the nutrients their bodies require. The following advice is emphasized for pre-planning meals and snacks:

Plan Your Week's Worth Of Dinners And Snacks

Every week, set aside some time to prepare your meals and snacks. This will keep you organized and guarantee that you have all the necessary components on hand.

Create A Shopping List

Make a grocery inventory after deciding on your meals and snacks for the week. By doing this, you can prevent making impulsive purchases and make sure you have everything you need to prepare wholesome dinners and snacks.

Prepare Your Food In Advance

Set aside some time each week to prepare your food. This might entail roasting poultry, cooking whole grains, or chopping veggies. By doing this, you can save time during the week and make sure that you always have wholesome dinners and snacks on hand.

Keep healthy snacks on hand so that you can satisfy your hunger when it hits. Fresh fruit, diced vegetables, nuts, and seeds are some examples of healthy snack choices.

Don't be hesitant to use leftovers; doing so can help you save time and guarantee that you have wholesome meals available at all times. Use the leftovers from your meals for lunches or dinners all week long by preparing additional servings.

It's crucial to be adaptable when it comes to meal preparation. Life occurs, so occasionally you might need to adjust your meal plan. Don't worry about it; just make the necessary adjustments and make an effort to eat as healthy as feasible.

Try Out New Recipes

Keeping motivated and engaged in your healthy eating plan can be achieved by experimenting with new recipes. Look for and test out healthy dishes online or in cookbooks.

Beginners with breast cancer can remain on track with their diet and make sure they are getting the nutrients their bodies require to stay healthy by adhering to these suggestions. Even though it may require a little additional work, planning meals and snacks in advance can be an effective tool for achieving and sustaining good health.

MEAL PLANS AND TREATMENTS FOR PATIENTS WITH DIFFERENT TYPES OF BREAST CANCER

As each person's needs may vary depending on their type of breast cancer, cancer stage, treatment plan, and general health status, it's essential to note that there isn't a meal plan that works for all breast cancer patients. Here are some basic recommendations for meal planning for patients with various forms of breast cancer and their treatments:

Prep Meal Schedule

Maintaining a healthy diet prior to surgery is crucial to preparing the body for the stress of the procedure and supporting the recovery process. For breast cancer patients preparing for surgery, the following meal schedule is recommended:

Oatmeal with fruit, almonds, and low-fat milk for breakfast.

Hummus and carrot spears for a snack.

Lunch will be grilled chicken salad with a side of quinoa, mixed vegetables, and avocado.

Greek yogurt and cut peaches for a snack.

Brown rice and baked salmon with roasted veggies for dinner.

Meal Plan for Chemotherapy

Chemotherapy side effects like sickness, vomiting, and appetite loss can make it challenging for patients to keep up a healthy diet. For those receiving chemotherapy for breast cancer, the following meal schedule is appropriate:

Smoothie for breakfast prepared with berries, spinach, chia seeds, and low-fat yogurt.

Apple slices with nut butter for a snack.

Lunch: A grilled chicken sandwich on whole wheat bread with avocado, tomato, and mixed vegetables.

Rice cakes with hummus and cucumber slices for a snack.

Dinner will be a stir-fry of vegetables, brown rice, and tofu.

Food Plan for Hormonal Therapy

Patients with hormone receptor-positive breast cancer frequently receive hormonal medication as a form of treatment. For those receiving hormonal therapy for breast cancer, the following meal plan is appropriate:

Breakfast would consist of avocado bread with a poached egg.

Greek yogurt, sliced almonds, and fruit for a snack.

Lunch will be a whole wheat turkey and cheese sandwich with baby vegetables on the side.

Hummus, whole grain crackers, and chopped bell peppers make a tasty snack.

Dinner will be fish on the grill with quinoa and roasted veggies.

Meal Plan for Radiation Therapy

Patients may find it challenging to maintain a healthy diet due to the side effects of radiation treatment, which include fatigue and skin irritation. Radiation treatment patients with breast cancer can use the following meal plan:

sliced banana, walnuts, and whole grain porridge for breakfast.

Apple segments with almond butter as a snack.

Lunch will be a wrap with turkey and cheese, mixed vegetables, avocado, and a fruit salad on the side.

Trail mix with nuts and dried berries for a snack.

Dinner will be roasted sweet potatoes, green beans, and baked poultry.

CHAPTER 9

LIFESTYLE CHANGES FOR PREVENTING AND CONTROLLING BREAST CANCER

Although there is no guarantee that breast cancer can be prevented, there are some lifestyle changes that can help lower the chance of getting the disease or speed up the healing process. These adjustments include changing to a healthy diet, getting regular exercise, keeping a healthy weight, consuming less booze, quitting smoking, and managing stress.

Healthy Eating: Preventing and treating breast cancer both require a healthy diet. Breast cancer risk can be decreased by consuming a diet high in fruits, veggies, whole grains, and lean protein. Specifically, cruciferous vegetables (like broccoli, kale, and cauliflower), berries, flaxseed, and fish are some foods that may be helpful. Limiting the intake of processed and red meat, sweetened beverages, and foods high in fat is also essential.

Exercise on a regular basis: Exercise is crucial for keeping general health and can help lower the risk of breast cancer. At least 150 minutes of moderate-intensity exercise or 75 minutes of vigorous-intensity exercise should be completed each week. This can include exercises like jogging, cycling, swimming, or brisk strolling.

Healthy Weight: Retaining a healthy weight is crucial for both preventing and recovering from breast cancer. Obesity can decrease the efficacy of treatment and increase the risk of breast cancer recurrence. Healthy eating and frequent exercise can help a person reach a healthy weight.

Limiting Alcohol Use: Drinking alcohol has been associated with a higher risk of getting breast cancer. One drink per day is the maximum amount of alcohol that women should consume, and it is advised that they abstain from alcohol entirely while receiving cancer therapy.

Avoiding Tobacco Use: Smoking has been associated with a higher chance of breast cancer and other cancers. Women should abstain from smoking and passive smoking.

Managing Stress Levels: Stress can be harmful to one's general health and can make breast cancer signs worse. Deep breathing exercises, yoga, meditation, and other tension-relieving practices can help control stress levels.

Along with making these lifestyle adjustments, it's critical for women to regularly undergo breast cancer tests like mammograms and clinical breast exams. For women with breast cancer, early detection and treatment can greatly improve outcomes.

Altering one's lifestyle can lower the chance of breast cancer and speed recovery. A healthcare professional should be consulted for specific advice and suggestions.

It's crucial to begin slowly and gradually increase the intensity and length of exercise for breast cancer patients and survivors as tolerated. Working with a physical therapist or certified exercise expert who can create a safe and effective exercise program customized to meet individual requirements may be necessary in this situation.

BENEFICIAL EXERCISE FOR PATIENTS AND SURVIVORS OF BREAST CANCER

The following exercises are possible benefits for breast cancer patients and survivors:

Walking: Walking is a low-impact activity that can practically be done anywhere and is simple to adapt to different fitness levels.

Yoga: Yoga can aid in increasing muscle, balance, and flexibility while also encouraging relaxation and stress relief.

Swimming: A low-impact activity that can help strengthen muscles and enhance cardiovascular health is swimming.

Resistance training: Exercises that increase bone density and keep muscle mass include using resistance bands or lifting weights.

Pilates: This low-impact activity can strengthen your core and increase your flexibility.

To maximize the advantages of breast cancer prevention and recovery, exercise should be combined with other lifestyle modifications like keeping a healthy diet, quitting smoking, and consuming less alcohol.

A crucial lifestyle change that can lower the chance of breast cancer and improve outcomes for those who have already been diagnosed with the disease is regular exercise. Patients and survivors of breast cancer can create a safe and efficient exercise program that is suited to their particular needs and objectives by working with a healthcare professional or certified exercise specialist.

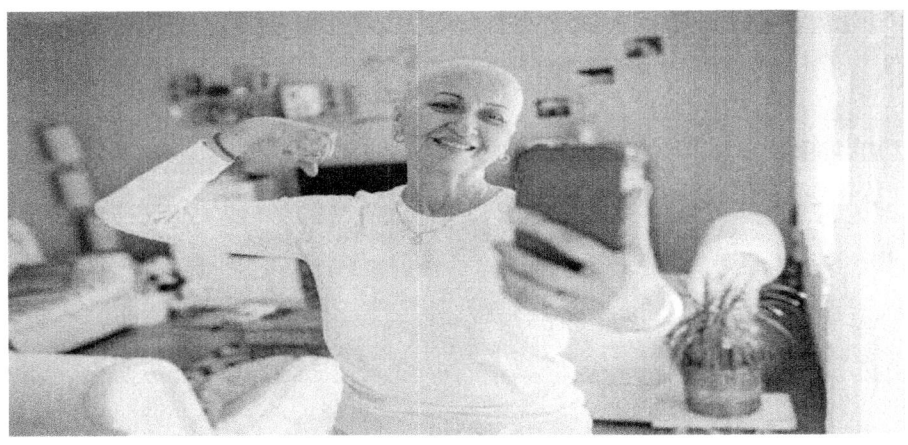

CONCLUSION

A serious illness that affects many individuals worldwide is breast cancer. While there is no foolproof method to ward off breast cancer, there are numerous lifestyle changes that can lower the chance of contracting the illness and enhance prognoses for those who have already been diagnosed. For breast cancer prevention and healing, it's crucial to maintain a healthy diet full of nutrients, such as protein, fiber, healthy fats, vitamins, and minerals. It can be easier to make sure that patients are getting the nutrients they need to keep their health by planning meals and snacks ahead of time. Exercise is also essential because it can improve immune system performance, lower inflammation, and control hormone levels. Breast cancer patients and survivors can enhance their general health and wellbeing, lower their chance of recurrence, and improve their quality of life by implementing these lifestyle changes. To create a customized strategy that addresses specific needs and goals, it is crucial to consult with licensed healthcare professionals and certified specialists. After receiving a breast cancer diagnosis, it is possible to lead a healthy and happy life with hard work and commitment.

BONUS

70 DAYS MEAL PLAN

Week 1

Day 1

Breakfast: Greek yogurt with blueberries and almonds

Snack: Carrots with hummus

Lunch: Grilled chicken salad with mixed greens, cherry tomatoes, cucumber, and balsamic vinaigrette

Snack: Apple slices with peanut butter

Dinner: Salmon with roasted asparagus and quinoa

Day 2

Breakfast: Spinach and mushroom omelet with whole-grain toast

Snack: Pear slices with cottage cheese

Lunch: Tuna salad sandwich on whole-grain bread with lettuce and tomato

Snack: Edamame

Dinner: Turkey meatballs with zucchini noodles and marinara sauce

Day 3

Breakfast: Overnight oats with banana and walnuts

Snack: String cheese with grapes

Lunch: Grilled vegetable and chicken skewers with brown rice

Snack: Trail mix with nuts and dried fruit

Dinner: Grilled steak with roasted brussels sprouts and sweet potato

Day 4

Breakfast: Whole-grain waffles with berries and almond butter

Snack: Yogurt with granola

Lunch: Lentil soup with whole-grain crackers

Snack: Sliced bell pepper with tzatziki

Dinner: Baked chicken with roasted carrots and cauliflower

Day 5

Breakfast: Smoothie with spinach, banana, almond milk, and protein powder

Snack: Hard-boiled egg with celery sticks

Lunch: Grilled portobello mushroom burger with sweet potato fries

Snack: Cherry tomatoes with mozzarella cheese

Dinner: Baked salmon with quinoa and roasted green beans

Day 6

Breakfast: Scrambled eggs with avocado and whole-grain toast

Snack: Apple slices with almond butter

Lunch: Greek salad with grilled chicken and whole-grain pita

Snack: Trail mix with nuts and dried fruit

Dinner: Turkey chili with mixed vegetables and brown rice

Day 7

Breakfast: Greek yogurt with berries and granola

Snack: Carrots with hummus

Lunch: Grilled chicken Caesar salad with whole-grain croutons

Snack: Hard-boiled egg with cucumber slices

Dinner: Baked cod with roasted asparagus and quinoa

Week 2

Day 1

Breakfast: Smoothie Bowl

Ingredients

1 cup of mixed berries (strawberries, blueberries, raspberries)

1 banana

1/2 cup of almond milk

1 scoop of protein powder

1 tablespoon of chia seeds

1/4 cup of granola

Instructions:

Blend the mixed berries, banana, almond milk, and protein powder in a blender until smooth.

Pour the mixture into a bowl.

Top with chia seeds and granola.

Prep time: 5 minutes

Snack: Apple slices with almond butter

Ingredients:

1 apple

2 tablespoons of almond butter

Instructions:

Cut the apple into slices.

Spread almond butter on the apple slices.

Prep time: 5 minutes

Lunch: Quinoa Salad

Ingredients:

1 cup of cooked quinoa

1/2 cup of cucumber, diced

1/2 cup of cherry tomatoes, halved

1/4 cup of red onion, diced

1/4 cup of feta cheese

2 tablespoons of olive oil

2 tablespoons of lemon juice

Salt and pepper to taste

Instructions:

In a large bowl, combine cooked quinoa, cucumber, cherry tomatoes, red onion, and feta cheese.

In a small bowl, whisk together olive oil, lemon juice, salt, and pepper.

Pour the dressing over the salad and toss to combine.

Prep time: 15 minutes

Snack: Carrot sticks with hummus

Ingredients:

1 cup of carrot sticks

1/4 cup of hummus

Instructions:

Wash and cut the carrots into sticks.

Serve with hummus for dipping.

Prep time: 5 minutes

Dinner: Grilled Salmon with Roasted Vegetables

Ingredients:

4 oz. of salmon fillet

1/2 cup of asparagus, trimmed

1/2 cup of broccoli florets

1/2 cup of cherry tomatoes, halved

1 tablespoon of olive oil

Salt and pepper to taste

Instructions:

Preheat the oven to 400°F (200°C).

On a baking sheet, toss asparagus, broccoli florets, and cherry tomatoes with olive oil, salt, and pepper.

Bake for 20-25 minutes or until the vegetables are tender.

Heat a grill pan over medium-high heat.

Season the salmon fillet with salt and pepper and grill for 3-4 minutes per side, or until cooked through.

Serve the salmon with the roasted vegetables on the side.

Prep time: 25 minutes

Cover the jar and refrigerate overnight.

In the morning, top with mixed berries.

Day 2

Breakfast: Smoothie made with almond milk, frozen mango, kale, and Greek yogurt

Lunch: Greek salad with grilled chicken, cucumbers, tomatoes, and feta cheese

Dinner: Lentil soup with whole grain bread

Day 3

Breakfast: Scrambled eggs with whole grain toast and sliced avocado

Lunch: Tuna salad with mixed greens, sliced cucumber, and whole grain crackers

Dinner: Grilled chicken with roasted asparagus and sweet potatoes

Day 4

Breakfast: Greek yogurt with mixed berries and chopped almonds

Lunch: Spinach salad with grilled shrimp, cherry tomatoes, and light vinaigrette

Dinner: Grilled salmon with roasted brussels sprouts and quinoa

Day 5

Breakfast: Smoothie made with almond milk, banana, peanut butter, and spinach

Lunch: Chicken and vegetable soup with whole grain crackers

Dinner: Lean beef stir-fry with mixed veggies and brown rice

Day 6

Breakfast: Oatmeal with diced apples, cinnamon, and almond milk

Lunch: Turkey and avocado wrap with whole grain tortilla, sliced tomato, and spinach

Dinner: Baked sweet potato with black beans, diced tomatoes, and guacamole

Day 7

Breakfast: Smoothie made with almond milk, frozen berries, kale, and Greek yogurt

Lunch: Quinoa and black bean salad with diced peppers, tomatoes, and avocado.

Week 3

Day 1

Breakfast - Green smoothie bowl: Blend together spinach, kale, banana, almond milk, and protein powder. Top with sliced strawberries, chia seeds, and sliced almonds.

Snack - Carrots and hummus.

Lunch - Grilled chicken salad with mixed greens, cherry tomatoes, avocado, and a balsamic vinaigrette.

Snack - Greek yogurt with mixed berries and honey.

Dinner - Grilled salmon with roasted Brussels sprouts and quinoa.

Day 2

Breakfast - Scrambled eggs with spinach and feta cheese, whole grain toast, and sliced tomatoes.

Snack - Apple slices with almond butter.

Lunch - Tuna salad on whole grain bread with mixed greens and cherry tomatoes.

Snack - Edamame.

Dinner - Baked chicken breast with roasted sweet potato and green beans.

Day 3

Breakfast - Smoothie bowl with mixed berries, Greek yogurt, almond milk, and granola.

Snack - Cottage cheese with sliced peaches.

Lunch - Turkey and avocado wrap on a whole grain tortilla with mixed greens and cherry tomatoes.

Snack - Almonds.

Dinner - Grilled shrimp with zucchini noodles and tomato sauce.

Day 4

Breakfast - Whole grain oatmeal with sliced bananas and walnuts.

Snack - Greek yogurt with mixed berries and honey.

Lunch - Grilled chicken breast with mixed greens, cherry tomatoes, and avocado.

Snack - Carrots and hummus.

Dinner - Baked salmon with roasted asparagus and brown rice.

Day 5

Breakfast - Vegetable and cheese omelet with whole grain toast.

Snack - Pear slices with almond butter.

Lunch - Grilled chicken Caesar salad with mixed greens and cherry tomatoes.

Snack - Edamame.

Dinner - Baked sweet potato with black bean chili.

Day 6

Breakfast - Greek yogurt with mixed berries, granola, and honey.

Snack - Apple slices with almond butter.

Lunch - Turkey and Swiss cheese sandwich on whole grain bread with mixed greens and cherry tomatoes.

Snack - Carrots and hummus.

Dinner - Grilled chicken with roasted broccoli and sweet potato fries.

Day 7

Breakfast - Whole grain waffles with mixed berries and Greek yogurt.

Snack - Cottage cheese with sliced peaches.

Lunch - Tuna salad on whole grain bread with mixed greens and cherry tomatoes.

Snack - Almonds.

Dinner - Grilled salmon with roasted Brussels sprouts and quinoa.

Week 4

Day 1

Breakfast

Overnight oats with mixed berries and chopped nuts (prep time: 5 minutes)

Green tea

Snack

Carrots and hummus (prep time: 5 minutes)

Lunch

Quinoa salad with mixed greens, cherry tomatoes, sliced cucumbers, and balsamic vinaigrette dressing (prep time: 20 minutes)

Whole grain crackers (prep time: 2 minutes)

Snack

Apple slices with 1 tablespoon almond butter (prep time: 5 minutes)

Dinner

Grilled chicken breast with lemon and herb seasoning (prep time: 20 minutes)

Roasted sweet potatoes and green beans (prep time: 25 minutes)

Snack

Greek yogurt with mixed berries and chopped nuts (prep time: 5 minutes)

Day 2

Breakfast

Berry and banana smoothie: blend 1 cup mixed berries, 1 banana, 1 cup almond milk, and 1 scoop vanilla protein powder (prep time: 5 minutes)

Whole grain toast with 1 tablespoon almond butter and sliced banana (prep time: 5 minutes)

Snack

Edamame (prep time: 5 minutes)

Lunch

Tuna salad with mixed greens, cherry tomatoes, sliced cucumbers, and olive oil-based dressing (prep time: 20 minutes)

Whole grain crackers (prep time: 2 minutes)

Snack

Peach slices with 1 tablespoon almond butter (prep time: 5 minutes)

Dinner

Baked salmon with lemon and dill seasoning (prep time: 20 minutes)

Roasted Brussels sprouts and carrots (prep time: 25 minutes)

Snack

Greek yogurt with mixed berries and chopped nuts (prep time: 5 minutes

Day 3

Breakfast

Veggie omelette: whisk 2 eggs with chopped spinach, mushrooms, and onions, cook on stovetop (prep time: 10 minutes)

Whole grain toast (prep time: 2 minutes)

Snack

Cherry tomatoes and mozzarella cheese (prep time: 5 minutes)

Lunch

Lentil soup with mixed greens (prep time: 25 minutes)

Whole grain crackers (prep time: 2 minutes)

Snack

Pear slices with 1 tablespoon almond butter (prep time: 5 minutes)

Dinner

Grilled chicken kebab with mixed veggies (bell peppers, onions, and mushrooms) and olive oil-based marinade (prep time: 25 minutes)

Quinoa (prep time: 15 minutes)

Snack

Greek yogurt with mixed berries and chopped nuts (prep time: 5 minutes)

Day 4

Breakfast

Greek yogurt with mixed berries and chopped nuts (prep time: 5 minutes)

Whole grain toast with avocado and cherry tomatoes (prep time: 5 minutes)

Snack

Celery and peanut butter (prep time: 5 minutes)

Lunch

Grilled chicken salad with mixed greens, cherry tomatoes, sliced cucumbers, and balsamic vinaigrette dressing (prep time: 15 minutes)

Whole grain crackers (prep time: 2 minutes)

Snack

Orange slices with 1 tablespoon almond butter (prep time: 5 minutes)

Dinner

Baked salmon with honey and garlic glaze (prep time: 20 minutes)

Steamed asparagus (prep time: 10 minutes)

Brown rice (prep time: 25 minutes)

Snack

Greek yogurt with mixed berries and chopped nuts (prep time

Week 5

Day 1

Breakfast: Greek yogurt with chopped almonds and berries

Lunch: Turkey and avocado wrap with whole grain tortilla, sliced tomato, and spinach

Dinner: Grilled salmon with roasted asparagus and quinoa

Day 2

Breakfast: Smoothie made with almond milk, banana, spinach, and chia seeds

Lunch: Mixed greens salad with grilled chicken, cherry tomatoes, cucumbers, and balsamic vinaigrette

Dinner: Whole wheat spaghetti with homemade marinara sauce, lean ground turkey, and sautéed veggies

Day 3

Breakfast: Oatmeal with diced apples, cinnamon, and almond milk

Lunch: Tuna salad with mixed greens, sliced cucumber, and whole grain crackers

Dinner: Baked sweet potato with black beans, diced tomatoes, and guacamole

Day 4

Breakfast: Scrambled eggs with whole grain toast and sliced avocado

Lunch: Chicken and vegetable soup with whole grain crackers

Dinner: Grilled chicken with roasted brussels sprouts and brown rice

Day 5

Breakfast: Smoothie made with almond milk, frozen berries, kale, and Greek yogurt

Lunch: Grilled vegetable wrap with hummus and whole grain tortilla

Dinner: Baked salmon with steamed broccoli and quinoa

Day 6

Breakfast: Greek yogurt with diced peaches and chopped walnuts

Lunch: Spinach salad with grilled shrimp, cherry tomatoes, and light vinaigrette

Dinner: Lean beef stir-fry with mixed veggies and brown rice

Day 7

Breakfast: Smoothie made with almond milk, frozen banana, peanut butter, and spinach

Lunch: Quinoa and black bean salad with diced peppers, tomatoes, and avocado

Dinner: Grilled chicken with roasted sweet potatoes and green beans

Week 6

Day 1

Breakfast: Oatmeal with diced pear, cinnamon, and almond milk

Lunch: Turkey and Swiss sandwich on whole grain bread with sliced tomato and lettuce

Dinner: Baked cod with steamed carrots and brown rice

Day 2

Breakfast: Smoothie made with almond milk, frozen mango, kale, and Greek yogurt

Lunch: Greek salad with grilled chicken, cucumbers, tomatoes, and feta cheese

Dinner: Lentil soup with whole grain bread

Day 3

Breakfast: Scrambled eggs with whole grain toast and sliced avocado

Lunch: Tuna salad with mixed greens, sliced cucumber, and whole grain crackers

Dinner: Grilled chicken with roasted asparagus and sweet potatoes

Day 4

Breakfast: Greek yogurt with mixed berries and chopped almonds

Lunch: Spinach salad with grilled shrimp, cherry tomatoes, and light vinaigrette

Dinner: Grilled salmon with roasted brussels sprouts and quinoa

Day 5

Breakfast: Smoothie made with almond milk, banana, peanut butter, and spinach

Lunch: Chicken and vegetable soup with whole grain crackers

Dinner: Lean beef stir-fry with mixed veggies and brown rice

Day 6

Breakfast: Oatmeal with diced apples, cinnamon, and almond milk

Lunch: Turkey and avocado wrap with whole grain tortilla, sliced tomato, and spinach

Dinner: Baked sweet potato with black beans, diced tomatoes, and guacamole

Day 7

Breakfast: Smoothie made with almond milk, frozen berries, kale, and Greek yogurt

Lunch: Quinoa and black bean salad with diced peppers, tomatoes, and avocado.

Week 7

Day 1

Breakfast: Strawberry and Banana Smoothie

1 banana

1 cup strawberries

1/2 cup Greek yogurt

1/2 cup almond milk

1 tsp honey

Blend all ingredients in a blender until smooth. Serve immediately.

Snack: Hummus and Carrots

2 tbsp hummus

1 cup baby carrots

Dip the carrots into the hummus and enjoy.

Lunch: Mediterranean Quinoa Salad

1 cup cooked quinoa

1/2 cup cherry tomatoes, halved

1/2 cup cucumber, chopped

1/4 cup kalamata olives, chopped

1/4 cup crumbled feta cheese

2 tbsp olive oil

1 tbsp lemon juice

Salt and pepper to taste

Mix all ingredients together in a large bowl. Serve chilled.

Snack: Apple slices with almond butter

1 apple, sliced

2 tbsp almond butter

Spread almond butter on apple slices and enjoy.

Dinner: Grilled Salmon with Asparagus

4 oz grilled salmon

1 cup grilled asparagus

1/2 cup quinoa, cooked

Salt and pepper to taste

Season the salmon and asparagus with salt and pepper. Grill the salmon and asparagus until fully cooked. Serve with quinoa on the side.

Day 2

Breakfast: Spinach and Mushroom Omelette

2 eggs

1/4 cup chopped spinach

1/4 cup sliced mushrooms

1/4 cup shredded cheddar cheese

Salt and pepper to taste

Whisk the eggs in a bowl and season with salt and pepper. In a nonstick pan, sauté the spinach and mushrooms until tender. Add the whisked eggs to the pan and cook until set. Sprinkle with cheese and fold the omelette in half.

Snack: Greek yogurt with berries

1/2 cup Greek yogurt

1/2 cup mixed berries

Mix the yogurt and berries together and enjoy.

Lunch: Chickpea Salad

1 can chickpeas, drained and rinsed

1/2 cup chopped cucumber

1/2 cup chopped tomato

1/4 cup chopped red onion

1/4 cup chopped parsley

2 tbsp olive oil

1 tbsp lemon juice

Salt and pepper to taste

Mix all ingredients together in a large bowl. Serve chilled.

Snack: Almonds and dried apricots

1/4 cup almonds

1/4 cup dried apricots

Combine the almonds and dried apricots and enjoy.

Dinner: Turkey and Vegetable Stir-Fry

4 oz ground turkey

1 cup mixed vegetables (broccoli, bell pepper, carrots)

1 tbsp olive oil

1 tbsp low-sodium soy sauce

Salt and pepper to taste

Heat the olive oil in a nonstick pan over medium heat. Add the ground turkey and cook until browned. Add the vegetables and soy sauce and stir-fry until tender. Season with salt and pepper to taste.

Day 3

Breakfast: Blueberry and Chia Seed Pudding

1/2 cup chia seeds

1 cup almond milk

1/2 cup blueberries

1 tsp honey

Mix the chia seeds and almond milk in a bowl and let sit in the refrigerator for at least 2 hours or overnight. Top with blueberries and drizzle with honey.

Week 8

Day 1

Breakfast: Greek yogurt with blueberries and almonds

Snack: Carrots with hummus

Lunch: Grilled chicken salad with mixed greens, cherry tomatoes, cucumber, and balsamic vinaigrette

Snack: Apple slices with peanut butter

Dinner: Salmon with roasted asparagus and quinoa

Day 2

Breakfast: Spinach and mushroom omelet with whole-grain toast

Snack: Pear slices with cottage cheese

Lunch: Tuna salad sandwich on whole-grain bread with lettuce and tomato

Snack: Edamame

Dinner: Turkey meatballs with zucchini noodles and marinara sauce

Day 3

Breakfast: Overnight oats with banana and walnuts

Snack: String cheese with grapes

Lunch: Grilled vegetable and chicken skewers with brown rice

Snack: Trail mix with nuts and dried fruit

Dinner: Grilled steak with roasted brussels sprouts and sweet potato

Day 4

Breakfast: Whole-grain waffles with berries and almond butter

Snack: Yogurt with granola

Lunch: Lentil soup with whole-grain crackers

Snack: Sliced bell pepper with tzatziki

Dinner: Baked chicken with roasted carrots and cauliflower

Day 5

Breakfast: Smoothie with spinach, banana, almond milk, and protein powder

Snack: Hard-boiled egg with celery sticks

Lunch: Grilled portobello mushroom burger with sweet potato fries

Snack: Cherry tomatoes with mozzarella cheese

Dinner: Baked salmon with quinoa and roasted green beans

Day 6

Breakfast: Scrambled eggs with avocado and whole-grain toast

Snack: Apple slices with almond butter

Lunch: Greek salad with grilled chicken and whole-grain pita

Snack: Trail mix with nuts and dried fruit

Dinner: Turkey chili with mixed vegetables and brown rice

Day 7

Breakfast: Greek yogurt with berries and granola

Snack: Carrots with hummus

Lunch: Grilled chicken Caesar salad with whole-grain croutons

Snack: Hard-boiled egg with cucumber slices

Dinner: Baked cod with roasted asparagus and quinoa

Week 9

Day 1

Breakfast: Omelet with spinach, mushrooms, and feta cheese

Snack: Apple slices with peanut butter

Lunch: Grilled shrimp salad with mixed greens, cherry tomatoes, cucumber, and balsamic vinaigrette

Snack: Edamame

Dinner: Baked chicken with roasted brussels sprouts and sweet potato

Day 2

Breakfast: Smoothie with kale, banana, almond milk, and protein powder

Snack: Greek yogurt with berries

Lunch: Turkey and avocado wrap with whole-grain tortilla

Snack: Trail mix with nuts and dried fruit

Dinner: Grilled steak with roasted asparagus and quinoa

Day 3

Breakfast: Whole-grain pancakes with blueberries and almond butter

Snack: Carrots with hummus

Lunch: Grilled vegetable and chicken skewers with brown rice

Snack: String cheese with grapes

Dinner: Baked salmon with roasted brussels sprouts and sweet potato

Day 4

Breakfast: Greek yogurt with berries and granola

Snack: Apple slices with almond butter

Lunch: Quinoa and black bean salad with mixed greens and avocado

Snack: Edamame

Dinner: Grilled chicken with roasted asparagus and quino

Day 5

Breakfast: Greek yogurt with berries and granola

Snack: Carrots with hummus

Lunch: Grilled chicken Caesar salad with whole-grain croutons

Snack: Hard-boiled egg with cucumber slices

Dinner: Baked cod with roasted asparagus and quinoa

Week 10

Day 1

Breakfast - Green smoothie bowl: Blend together spinach, kale, banana, almond milk, and protein powder. Top with sliced strawberries, chia seeds, and sliced almonds.

Snack - Carrots and hummus.

Lunch - Grilled chicken salad with mixed greens, cherry tomatoes, avocado, and a balsamic vinaigrette.

Snack - Greek yogurt with mixed berries and honey.

Dinner - Grilled salmon with roasted Brussels sprouts and quinoa.

Day 2

Breakfast - Scrambled eggs with spinach and feta cheese, whole grain toast, and sliced tomatoes.

Snack - Apple slices with almond butter.

Lunch - Tuna salad on whole grain bread with mixed greens and cherry tomatoes.

Snack - Edamame.

Dinner - Baked chicken breast with roasted sweet potato and green beans.

Day 3

Breakfast - Smoothie bowl with mixed berries, Greek yogurt, almond milk, and granola.

Snack - Cottage cheese with sliced peaches.

Lunch - Turkey and avocado wrap on a whole grain tortilla with mixed greens and cherry tomatoes.

Snack - Almonds.

Dinner - Grilled shrimp with zucchini noodles and tomato sauce.

Day 4

Breakfast - Whole grain oatmeal with sliced bananas and walnuts.

Snack - Greek yogurt with mixed berries and honey.

Lunch - Grilled chicken breast with mixed greens, cherry tomatoes, and avocado.

Snack - Carrots and hummus.

Dinner - Baked salmon with roasted asparagus and brown rice.

Day 5

Breakfast - Vegetable and cheese omelet with whole grain toast.

Snack - Pear slices with almond butter.

Lunch - Grilled chicken Caesar salad with mixed greens and cherry tomatoes.

Snack - Edamame.

Dinner - Baked sweet potato with black bean chili.

Day 6

Breakfast - Greek yogurt with mixed berries, granola, and honey.

Snack - Apple slices with almond butter.

Lunch - Turkey and Swiss cheese sandwich on whole grain bread with mixed greens and cherry tomatoes.

Snack - Carrots and hummus.

Dinner - Grilled chicken with roasted broccoli and sweet potato fries.

Day 7

Breakfast - Whole grain waffles with mixed berries and Greek yogurt.

Snack - Cottage cheese with sliced peaches.

Lunch - Tuna salad on whole grain bread with mixed greens and cherry tomatoes.

Snack - Almonds.

Dinner - Grilled salmon with roasted Brussels sprouts and quinoa.

Printed in Great Britain
by Amazon

24113317R00090